TEACHER'S GUIDE

In No Time Flat!

Christine Root   Karen Blanchard

DELTA PUBLISHING COMPANY

DELTA PUBLISHING COMPANY
A DIVISION OF DELTA SYSTEMS COMPANY, INC.

1400 Miller Parkway
McHenry, IL 60050 USA
(815) 363–3582 Toll Free (800) 323–8270
www.delta–systems.com

Printed in the United States of America

10 9 8 7 6 5 4 3 2

Author: Christine Root
Karen Blanchard

ISBN 1–887744–35–5

CONTENTS

Introduction

UNIT ONE:
Lesson 1 2
Lesson 2 3
Lesson 3 4
Lesson 4 5
Lesson 5 6
Mid-Unit Review 7
Lesson 6 8
Lesson 7 9
Lesson 8 10
Lesson 9 11
Lesson 10 12
Unit One Review 13

UNIT TWO:
Lesson 11 16
Lesson 12 17
Lesson 13 18
Lesson 14 19
Lesson 15 20
Mid-Unit Review 21
Lesson 16 22
Lesson 17 23
Lesson 18 24
Lesson 19 25
Lesson 20 26
Unit Two Review 27

UNIT THREE:
Lesson 21 30
Lesson 22 31
Lesson 23 32
Lesson 24 33
Lesson 25 34
Mid-Unit Review 35
Lesson 26 36
Lesson 27 37
Lesson 28 38
Lesson 29 39
Lesson 30 40
Unit Three Review 41

Photocopiables 45-56

INTRODUCTION

Idioms and phrasal verbs are an integral part of the English language, but are among the most challenging aspects of learning English as a second or foreign language. This two-level low intermediate series is designed to help students develop their ability to recognize, understand and use high-frequency phrasal verbs and idioms in authentic contexts in both written and spoken form. The exercise types in this series take into consideration students' varying learning styles as well as providing practice in different skill areas.

The phrasal verbs and idioms presented in the series are those most commonly seen and heard in everyday conversations, both in professional and personal settings. In addition, phrasal verbs and idioms which have appeared in TOEFL tests are included.

To make the learning of idiomatic expressions a more manageable task, the series is divided into two levels: **Zero In! Phrasal Verbs in Context** and **In No Time Flat! Idioms in Context**. Phrasal verbs (i.e. *find out, give up*) are presented in the first level since students can quickly learn to identify the pattern "verb plus preposition." Idioms (i.e. *give me a hand, hit the roof*) provided in the second level are more difficult to master since there are no systematic patterns for students to learn. Within each level, the phrasal verbs and idioms are grouped according to semantic similarity, and are consistently reviewed and recycled.

LESSON OUTLINE: *Procedures*

In No Time Flat! Idioms in Context consists of 30, two-page lessons that are grouped into three units. Expressions are reviewed in a variety of exercises every five lessons. An additional two-page review occurs at the end of each unit.

Each of the 30 lessons is organized according to the following structure:

LEARN BY HEART

Each lesson introduces three or four idioms with clear definitions and example sentences. Sometimes idioms that have the same meaning are included in parentheses. For example:

walking on air (on cloud nine/in seventh heaven) – to be extremely happy because something great has happened

Some of the idioms are marked with *(my)**. This idicates that possessive adjectives *(my, your, his, her, our, their)* are to be used. For example:

I am really *up to my ears* in work. He is really *up to his ears* in work...

- Have students read through the definition and example sentence of the first idiom silently.
- Review definition. Clarify meaning.
- Read the example sentences. Continue with other idioms.
- As an extension, teacher may have class write further example sentences.

The presentation and definition section is followed by three or four one-panel cartoons that illustrate the meaning of each idiom. Students are asked to write the appropriate idiom on the line below each cartoon. This process of looking at the cartoon, thinking about which idiom it represents, and finally writing the correct words on the line solidifies meanings in students' minds. The material is presented in more than one modality so that students with varying learning styles (i.e. visual, auditory, tactile) can all learn efficiently. By both seeing (a picture) and then writing (words), students use different learning modes.

- Have students work individually. Have them look at the cartoon and decide which idiom completes each statement.
- Compare answers with a partner.
- Go over the answers as a class.

USE YOUR HEAD

This section of the lesson provides exercises that give specific practice in understanding and using the expressions in authentic-type situations. The exercises and activities simulate real life situations and are personalized whenever possible. Students are asked in an identification exercise, for example, situations where they would *hold their tongue.* In another identification exercise, they are asked to list songs they know *by heart.* Likely answers for exercises are provided in the answer key, although responses may vary.

- Go through explanations in the student book. Have students work individually, in pairs, or in small groups, depending on the exercise.
- Discuss answers as a class.

PLAY IT BY EAR

A listening exercise is included at the end of each lesson since phrasals/idioms are so frequently used in conversations. These exercises take the form of short dialogs or reading passages followed by comprehension questions. The purpose is to give students practice in hearing the phrasals/idioms used in natural speech.

- Play the tape. Have students listen for answers.
- Discuss answers as a class. Teacher may choose to play the tape again.

REVIEW LESSONS

The phrasals and idioms are recycled throughout the text. The idioms are reviewed at the end of every five lessons. The review includes exercises in contrasting the meanings of the various idioms by picking out synonyms and antonyms, choosing correct definitions, answering questions that require an understanding of the expression at hand, and using the correct expressions in dialogs.

- Have students complete the exercises individually or in pairs. (Teacher may also want to assign this as a homework assignment.)
- Discuss answers as a class.

A two-page review also occurs at the end of each unit. In this 10-lesson review, students are required to show their understanding of the different idioms presented. They are asked to fill in the blanks using idioms from that unit.

- Have students complete the review individually. (Teacher may also want to assign this as a homework assignment.)
- Discuss answers as a class.

EXTENSION IDEAS

Personal Dictionary

Have students record idioms from each lesson in a personal dictionary. Have them write example sentences that explain the meaning of the idioms in a context that is relevant to their situation.

Class Cartoons

Have students work in pairs or small groups to design cartoons that depict one of the idioms introduced in that lesson. As in *Get the Picture,* students can leave blanks and let their classmates complete the statements. Cartoons can be displayed in the classroom.

Role Play

In pairs or small groups, brainstorm a situation that could involve one of the idioms introduced in that lesson. Write up a short dialog. Confirm understanding by concluding with a question using that idiom. Share dialogs with other groups or perform for the class. For example:

Man 1: *What's wrong with you, James?*

Man 2: *I'm really angry at Mark.*

Man 1: *Why is that?*

Man 2: *I told him that I was planning to move to New York but I asked him to keep it a secret. He told a lot of people, including my boss.*

Man 1: *Oh no! Never tell Mark a secret! He always tells.*

Question: Did Mark *spill the beans* about James?

ADDITIONAL PRACTICE

Journal Writing

Teachers may want to have students write a paragraph or other type of writing passage highlighting the use of one of that lesson's idioms. Teachers can adapt activities to have students work individually or in pairs or small groups.

- Have students brainstorm ideas using simple charts. Photocopiables are provided for each lesson in the back of the Teacher's Guide. (Teachers may also choose to draw these on the board for students to copy into their books.) Teacher can go around the class and check students' charts. Emphasize the use of the idioms in questioning them about their choices.
- Have students write up ideas in paragraphs. Final work could be presented in individual journals or as a group presentation in front of the class.

Lessons 1–10

GET THE PICTURE

1. Mrs. Perkins was very **nosy.** She always knew what was happening.
2. Tim was **up to his ears** in dirty dishes.
3. Sammy the cat **kept an eye on** Tramp the dog.

USE YOUR HEAD

Answers will vary for some exercises. Likely answers are provided.

A. 1. yes; 2. yes; 3. no
B. 1. children; 2. clock; 3. road; 4. ball
C. Answers will vary.
D. Answers will vary.

PLAY IT BY EAR

1. a; 2. c; 3. b

TAPESCRIPT:

Conversation 1

M: *Would you like to go out to lunch today? There's a new Chinese restaurant in town that's very good.*
W: *I'd love to, but I'm* **up to my ears** *in work this week.*
M: *Maybe we can go next week then.*
W: *That sounds great.*
1. Why can't the woman go out to lunch?

Conversation 2

M: *I met your next-door neighbor, Mrs. Tabis, at a party last night.*
W: *Really? I try to avoid her. She always asks so many personal questions.*
M: *I know what you mean. She asked me quite a few questions and I had just met her.*
2. What do people think of Mrs. Tabis?

Conversation 3

W1: *I have to work late tonight. Do you think you could* **keep an eye on** *my kids until I get home?*
W2: *No problem.*
W1: *They get home from school at 3:30 and I'll be back around 7:00.*
W2: *That sounds fine. I'll see you tonight.*
3. What does the woman want her friend to do?

ADDITIONAL PRACTICE

See photocopiable on page 42.

GET THE PICTURE

1. Rush hour traffic jams can be **a pain in the neck.**
2. "When Dwayne told me he used to play guitar with the Rolling Stones, I knew he was **pulling my leg.**"
3. Donna had to **twist her arm** to get Lynn to the popcorn stand.

USE YOUR HEAD

A. 1. yes; 2. yes; 3. no; 4. yes
B. Answers will vary.
C. Answers will vary.
D. Answers will vary.

PLAY IT BY EAR

1. F; 2. T; 3. F

TAPESCRIPT:

Situation 1

W: *"When Sarah told me that she had a date with Brad Pitt, I knew she was* **pulling my leg.** *I'm sure she's never even met him."*

Situation 2

M: *"I don't want to work with Tom anymore. He never finishes his work on time and always wants me to stay late and help him. He's* **a pain in the neck."**

Situation 3

M: *"I really don't like to lend anyone my car. But Frank really* **twisted my arm** *and I finally agreed. I hope he's careful with it."*

ADDITIONAL PRACTICE

See photocopiable on page 42.

GET THE PICTURE

1. "In this job, you really have to be **on your toes** at all times."
2. The math assignment was **over his head.**
3. "Thanks for agreeing to **foot the bill** for the ice cream, Dad!"

USE YOUR HEAD

A. 1. no; 2. yes; 3. yes; 4. no; 5. yes; 6. yes
B. Answers will vary. (Could include *filling up the car with gas, taking in the car for a tune-up, checking the tires, studying a map, preparing a snack,* etc.)
C. Answers will vary.
Answers will vary. (Could include *gift, renting a hall, decorations, drinks,* etc.)
D. Answers will vary.

PLAY IT BY EAR

1. c; 2. c; 3. a

TAPESCRIPT:

Conversation 1

M: How do you like your French course?
W: The teacher is great, but the course is really **over my head.**
M: Do you think you'll pass?
W: I'm not sure.
1. What does the woman think about her French course?

Conversation 2

M: I heard you're having a big graduation party for our whole class.
W: Yes, I hope you can come. It's a lot of work to plan, but it should be fun.
M: Who's doing all the organizing and planning?
W: I'm doing the planning, but my father is **footing the bill.**
2. Who is paying for the graduation party?

Conversation 3

W: How is your new job going?
M: It's not bad, but I really don't like working at night.
W: Why not?
M: It's hard to stay **on my toes** *when most people are sleeping!*
3. What is difficult for the man to do?

ADDITIONAL PRACTICE

See photocopiable on page 43.

GET THE PICTURE

1. Gary and Larry **saw eye to eye** on most things, including fashion.
2. "The costume party totally **slipped my mind.**"
3. "I think you'd better **hold your tongue.**"

USE YOUR HEAD

A. Answers will vary.
B. Answers will vary.
C. Answers will vary.

PLAY IT BY EAR

1. T; 2. F; 3. T

TAPESCRIPT:

Situation 1:

M: I promised my friend that I would give her a ride home from school. When I got home she called and asked me what had happened. She had been waiting for an hour. I felt terrible that I'd forgotten my promise. I told her that it had completely **slipped my mind.**

Situation 2:

W: Yesterday my brother was helping me with my math homework. He laughed at me when I didn't know how to do one of the problems. I wanted to yell at him, but I decided to **hold my tongue** *because I really needed his help.*

Situation 3:

W: My husband and I have three teenagers. They're good kids, but still it's a lot of work. Luckily, my husband and I **see eye to eye** *on how to raise them.*

ADDITIONAL PRACTICE

See photocopiable on page 43.

GET THE PICTURE

1. Ethel **kept her fingers crossed** that she'd get the right card.
2. "Remember to **keep your chin up!**"
3. Ella and Elmer were **head over heels in love.**

USE YOUR HEAD

A. Answers will vary.
B. 1. yes; 2. yes; 3. no; 4. yes
C. 1. yes; 2. no; 3. yes; 4. no; 5. yes

PLAY IT BY EAR

1. F; 2. T; 3. T

TAPESCRIPT:

Conversation:

W: My friend Alice fell **head over heels in love** *with a guy named Nathan who she met at work. She was* **keeping her fingers crossed** *that he would ask her out on a date. She waited for several months, but he never asked her out. Finally she found out that Nathan already had a girlfriend. She was upset, but I told her to* **keep her chin up.** *I'm sure she will meet someone else soon.*

1. Nathan fell in love with Alice.
2. Alice hoped that Nathan would ask her out on a date.
3. Alice's friend told her not to worry.

ADDITIONAL PRACTICE

See photocopiable on page 44.

A. 1. it **slipped my mind;** 2. we usually **see eye to eye;** 3. he will **foot the bill;** 4. she was **pulling my leg;** 5. he had to **twist my arm;** 6. I am going to **keep an eye on them;** 7. she is very **nosy;** 8. they are **head over heels in love;** 9. I **held my tongue;** 10. it was **over my head**

B. 1. no; 2. yes; 3. no; 4. no; 5. no

C. 1. My uncle is always **pulling my leg;** 2. I agreed to **foot the bill;** 3. This assignment is **over my head;** 4. My sister and I **see eye to eye** on important things; 5. I don't want to go out with Robert because he's **a pain in the neck**

GET THE PICTURE

1. Barry **got cold feet** and couldn't perform.
2. The car **cost an arm and a leg** but Mary wanted to have it.
3. Jason knew all the words of the play **by heart.**

USE YOUR HEAD

A. Answers will vary.
B. Answers will vary.
C. Answers will vary.
D. 1; 2; 4; 5; 6

PLAY IT BY EAR

1. a; 2. c; 3. b

TAPESCRIPT:

Situation 1:
M: "Keiko learned how to spell all of the vocabulary words **by heart.**"

Situation 2:
W: "Richard was supposed to sing a song in the concert tonight, but he **got cold feet** *at the last minute."*

Situation 3:
W: "The dress that I wanted to buy for the dance **cost an arm and a leg,** *so I borrowed one from my friend instead."*

ADDITIONAL PRACTICE

See photocopiable on page 44.

GET THE PICTURE

1. "Could I **give you a hand?**"
2. "Would you please **make up your mind?**"
3. The sound of Arnold's drums **got on their nerves.**"

USE YOUR HEAD

A. Answers will vary.
B. 1. Yes; 2. Yes; 3. Yes; 4. Yes; 5. No
C. Answers will vary.

PLAY IT BY EAR

1. She asked the man to help her carry her bags up the stairs.
2. She can't decide whether or not to accept the job that the bank offered her.
3. He is upset because his roommate is always borrowing things without asking him.

TAPESCRIPT:

Conversation 1

M: Wow! You've got a lot of bags. Did you just get back from the supermarket?
W: Yes. And the bags are quite heavy. Could you **give me a hand** *carrying them up the stairs?*
M: Sure. No problem.
1. What did the woman ask the man to do?

Conversation 2

M: Did you have that interview at the bank?
W: Yes. Actually, they offered me a job.
M: Great! Are you going to accept it?
W: I don't know. I still can't **make up my mind.**
2. What can't the woman decide?

Conversation 3

M1: How are you getting along with your new roommate?
M2: Not very well. He really **gets on my nerves.**
M1: What does he do?
M2: He always borrows my things without asking me.
3. Why is the man upset with his roommate?

ADDITIONAL PRACTICE

See photocopiable on page 45.

Lesson 8

GET THE PICTURE

1. Sarah always was a **levelheaded** person.
2. Gordon's life is usually relaxing. **On the other hand,** it can also be dangerous.
3. "**Off the top of my head,** I'd say about 300 are coming for lunch today."

USE YOUR HEAD

A. Answers will vary.
B. Answers will vary.
C. Answers will vary.

PLAY IT BY EAR

1. F; 2. F; 3. F

TAPESCRIPT:

Conversation 1
M: I have to call Neil. Do you know his phone number?
W: I can't remember it **off the top of my head.** *But here's a phone book. You can look it up.*

Conversation 2
M: Would you rather have dinner at Myrna's Cafe or Sam's Grill?
W: Well, Myrna's is closer and cheaper. **On the other hand,** *Sam's Grill has better food.*
M: Let's go to Sam's then. I'm really hungry.

Conversation 3
M: Hey, you got a new assistant recently, right?
W: Yes. Just last week.
M: How's she working out?
W: She's great. Our office is so crazy sometimes that we really needed someone **levelheaded.**

ADDITIONAL PRACTICE

See photocopiable on page 45.

GET THE PICTURE

1. "Can I call you back? I **have my hands full** right now."
2. "Do I know you? Your name is **on the tip of my tongue.**"
3. Sparky the cat knew he would have to **face the music** later but he wouldn't stop playing with the dogs.

USE YOUR HEAD

A. 1. **on the tip of my tongue;** 2. **off the top of my head;** 3. **on the tip of my tongue**
B. Answers will vary.
C. Answers will vary.

PLAY IT BY EAR

1. T; 2. T; 3. F

TAPESCRIPT:

Conversation

W: *When my husband and I decided to have 10 children, we didn't know how much work it would be. Now we have to* **face the music.** *We really* **have our hands full** *day and night. The last two were twins, so it's double work! There are so many children now that I sometimes get their names wrong. I'll look at one of them and his or her name will be right* **on the tip of the tongue,** *but then I'll forget!*

1. The woman and her husband are very busy with their children.
2. The woman realizes that they have to accept the consequences of having so many children.
3. The woman can always remember the names of her children.

ADDITIONAL PRACTICE

See photocopiable on page 46.

GET THE PICTURE

1. "Let's **keep in touch** with each other."
2. Robby **lost face** when he finished the race in second place.
3. It was the first time for the two to meet **face to face.**

USE YOUR HEAD

A. Answers will vary.
B. Answers will vary.
C. Answers will vary.
D. Answers will vary.

PLAY IT BY EAR

1. no; by phone; 2. He got caught cheating on an exam.

TAPESCRIPT:

Conversation 1

M: Whatever happened to your old college roommate?
W: She got married and moved to Miami.
M: Do you ever see her anymore?
W: Well, I rarely get to see her **face to face,** *but we still* **keep in touch.** *We talk on the phone at least once a month and send each other pictures of our families.*

1. Does the woman see her college roommate in person very often?
   How does the woman **keep in touch** with her college roommate?

Conversation 2

W2: Did you hear that Jeremy got kicked out of school?
W1: Yes. He got caught cheating on an exam and now he can't return to school until next semester.
W2: Oh no! He must feel so ashamed!
W1: Yeah. You know he really **lost face** *with his family and friends.*

2. Why did Jeremy lose the respect of his friends and family?

ADDITIONAL PRACTICE

See photocopiable on page 46.

Review (Lessons 6-10)

A. 1. Yes; 2. No; 3. Yes; 4. Yes; 5. Yes; 6. No; 7. No; 8. Yes; 9. No

B. 1. **face to face**; 2. **got cold feet**; 3. **over my head**; 4. **lost face**; 5. **face the music**

C. 1. g; 2. c; 3. e; 4. a; 5. f; 6. d; 7. b

Unit One Review

1. **keep an eye on**; 2. **by heart**; 3. **head over heels in love**; 4. **make up my mind**; 5. **over my head**; 6. **keep in touch with**; 7. **a pain in the neck**; 8. **on the tip of my tongue**; 9. **up to my ears**; 10. **give me a hand**; 11. **keep my fingers crossed**; 12. **hold my tongue**; 13. **pulling my leg**; 14. **on the other hand**; 15. **on my toes**; 16. **face to face**; 17. **see eye to eye**; 18. **cost an arm and a leg**; 19. **nosy**; 20. **off the top of my head**

Lessons 11-20

GET THE PICTURE

1. "You'll be happy you decided to take up weighlifting **in the long run.**"
2. **In the short run,** Paul enjoyed having his own credit card.
3. "I think it's time to **throw in the towel** and call the repair shop."

USE YOUR HEAD

A. Answers will vary.
B. 1. Consolidated Inc.; 2. Acme Ltd.; 3. Answers will vary.
C. 2; 4; 5
D. Answers will vary.

PLAY IT BY EAR

1. T; 2. T; 3. T

TAPESCRIPT:

Statement 1

M: "When Paul realized that no one at the meeting was going to accept his ideas, he **threw in the towel** *and left."*

Statement 2

W: "It might be difficult in the first few years, but David knew that he could make a success of his computer business **in the long run.**"

Statement 3

W: "I'm willing to lose some money **in the short run** *because I know that this will be a good investment in the future."*

ADDITIONAL PRACTICE

See photocopiable on page 47.

GET THE PICTURE

1. Bill sometimes found it difficult to be **a team player.**
2. Jenny was always **on the ball** in class.
3. On the ranch, Sherman the sheep dog **called the shots.**

USE YOUR HEAD

A. Answers will vary.
B. 3, 4, 5, 7, 8
C. Max and Zach
D. Answers will vary. (Could include *preparing a resume, wearing suitable clothes, learning about the company, arriving at the interview on time,* etc.)
Answers will vary. (Could include *calling friends in advance to check schedules, arranging a meeting place, deciding what to eat and drink, checking the weather report,* etc.)

PLAY IT BY EAR

1. b; 2. a; 3. b

TAPESCRIPT:

Statement 1
W: "My mother has a very strong personality. She **calls** *all* **the shots** *in our family."*

Statement 2
M: "I really enjoy working with David. He's easy to get along with and he's a real **team player.**"

Statement 3
W: "Betty is one of the best nurses in the hospital. She's really **on the ball.** *All of the patients and staff like her."*

ADDITIONAL PRACTICE

See photocopiable on page 47.

GET THE PICTURE

1. Pete really **lost his shirt** in his new business.
2. Harry will always go golfing **at the drop of a hat.**
3. For Clara, winning the contest was **a feather in her cap.**

USE YOUR HEAD

A. 1; 3; 4
B. Answers will vary.
C. Answers will vary.

PLAY IT BY EAR

1. He won a scholarship to a tennis camp; 2. fight; 3. Mr. Kramer lost a lot of money.

TAPESCRIPT:

Conversation 1

M: I'm so proud of my son. He won a scholarship to a tennis camp.
W: Good for him! That's a real **feather in his cap.**
1. Why is the man proud of his son?

Conversation 2

W1: Frank has a bad temper, doesn't he?
W2: Yes. He's ready to fight **at the drop of a hat.**
2. What is Frank ready to do **at the drop of a hat?**

Conversation 3

W: I feel bad for Mr. Kramer. His company is going out of business.
M: I know. I really feel sorry for him. I heard he **lost his shirt.**
3. Why does the man feel sorry for Mr. Kramer?

ADDITIONAL PRACTICE

See photocopiable on page 48.

GET THE PICTURE

1. "I wish I could **be in his shoes.**"
2. George got really **hot under the collar** when the waiter spilled the drink.
3. Justin prefers to travel **on a shoestring.**

USE YOUR HEAD

A. Answers will vary.
B. Answers will vary.
C. Answers will vary.
D. Answers will vary.
E. 1. yes; 2. yes; 3. yes; 4. no; 5. no; 6. yes

PLAY IT BY EAR

1. a; 2. b; 3. c

TAPESCRIPT:

Conversation 1:
M: "Ever since Harry lost most of his money in the stock market, he's had to live **on a shoestring.**"

Conversation 2:
W: "Beth's job is very demanding. She has to work seven days a week and her boss isn't very nice. I wouldn't want to be **in her shoes.**"

Conversation 3:
M: "The professor doesn't like students to question his ideas. He gets **hot under the collar** *when anyone disagrees with him."*

ADDITIONAL PRACTICE

See photocopiable on page 48.

GET THE PICTURE

1. "Have we met before? Your name **rings a bell.**"
2. "In this kitchen, Carl really **knows the ropes.**"
3. "Where's your mom? Maybe I'll **give her a ring.**"

USE YOUR HEAD

A. Answers will vary.
B. 1. **Give me a ring;** 2. **ring a bell**
C. Answers will vary.
D. Answers will vary.

PLAY IT BY EAR

1. b; 2. c; 3. a

TAPESCRIPT:

Statement 1
M: "I need directions to the party. I'll call you when I get home from work."

Statement 2
W: "Harry Baker? Hmmm. I think that name sounds familiar."

Statement 3
M: "I've worked here for seven years, so I can help you. I understand how things work around here."

ADDITIONAL PRACTICE

See photocopiable on page 49.

A. 1. **he is a team player;** 2. I can live **on a shoestring;** 3. it doesn't **ring a bell;** 4. I wouldn't want to **be in his shoes;** 5. he got **hot under the collar;** 6. she **lost her shirt;** 7. he **threw in the towel;** 8. he is **on the ball;** 9. I don't **call the shots;** 10. I'll **give you a ring**

B. 1. b; 2. e; 3. c; 4. d; 5. a

C. 1. a; 2. c; 3. b; 4. a; 5. b

GET THE PICTURE

1. Jason found a sport that was right **up his alley.**
2. Roy finally **got the picture.** Patty didn't want to see him anymore.
3. At the ranch, Dave felt like **a fish out of water.**

USE YOUR HEAD

A. Answers will vary.
B. Answers will vary.
C. 1. no; 2. yes; 3. no

PLAY IT BY EAR

1. b; 2. b; 3. a

TAPESCRIPT:

Statement 1
W: *"When I first moved to Mexico to study Spanish, I felt like* **a fish out of water.**"

Statement 2
M: *"After my teacher explained how to do the experiment, I finally* **got the picture.**"

Statement 3
W: *"I was excited when my friend invited me to go hiking with him. Outdoor activities are right* **up my alley.**"

ADDITIONAL PRACTICE

See photocopiable on page 49.

GET THE PICTURE

1. "We'll get married soon, but **keep it under your hat."**
2. Susan was **walking on air** after winning the race.
3. Grant **spilled the beans** about Beth's big mistake at work.

USE YOUR HEAD

A. 1. yes; 2. yes; 3. no; 4. yes; 5. no
B. 1. You **kept it under your hat;** 2. You **spilled the beans;** 3. You **spilled the beans;** 4. You **kept it under your hat**
C. Answers will vary.
D. Answers will vary.

PLAY IT BY EAR

1. information about the surprise party; 2. Yes; 3. She got accepted into college.

TAPESCRIPT:

Conversation 1

W: *I'm having a surprise birthday party for Patty next Saturday. If you see her, please don't mention it.*
M: *Don't worry. I'll* **keep it under my hat.**
1. What does the woman want the man to **keep it under his hat?**

Conversation 2

M: *The boss asked me not to tell Veronica that she was getting a big promotion.*
W: *You're not very good at keeping secrets.*
M: *I know. As soon as I saw her, I* **spilled the beans.**
2. Did the man tell Veronica the secret?

Conversation 3

W1: You look very happy today.
W2: I am. I've been **walking on air** *ever since I found out I got accepted into college.*
3. Why is the woman **walking on air?**

ADDITIONAL PRACTICE

See photocopiable on page 50.

GET THE PICTURE

1. After just a few days in business, Sandy's shoe business was **in the black.**
2. Anna was **green with envy** when she saw Carolyn's new hat.
3. Gordon couldn't understand why his business was **in the red.**

USE YOUR HEAD

A. Answers will vary.
B. 1. **in the red;** 2. **in the black**
C. $240; no

PLAY IT BY EAR

1. c; 2. b; 3. a

TAPESCRIPT:

Situation 1
M: "When Kevin asked Patty to marry him, Nathan was really jealous. He wanted to ask her too."

Situation 2
W: "Bob's company is doing great. He's making more money than he ever dreamed he would."

Situation 3
W: "I lost all my money on a bad business deal. I don't know how I'll manage to pay my bills."

ADDITIONAL PRACTICE

See photocopiable on page 50.

GET THE PICTURE

1. It was **a red-letter day** for Greg when he finally graduated from college.
2. Renting the car involved a lot of **red tape.**
3. "I told **a white lie.** I told him I liked his new outfit."

USE YOUR HEAD

A. 1. yes; 2. yes; 3. no; 4. yes; 5. yes; 6. no
B. 1. yes; 2. no; 3. yes; 4. yes; 5. no; 6. yes
C. Answers will vary.

PLAY IT BY EAR

1. F; 2. T; 3. T

TAPESCRIPT:

Conversation 1

M: Was it easy to get your visa renewed?
W: Not at all. There was a lot of **red tape** *involved.*

Conversation 2

M: Did you like the gift your aunt gave you for your birthday?
W: Not really, but of course I told her that I loved it.

Conversation 3

M1: Congratulations! I heard you won first place in the essay contest!
M2: Thanks. Yes! I was so surprised I won. I'll never forget that day!

ADDITIONAL PRACTICE

See photocopiable on page 51.

Lesson 20

GET THE PICTURE

1. Beatrice dropped by for a visit **out of the blue.**
2. Will spends all day at the office. He is **a white-collar worker.**
3. Jonathan got a haircut **once in a blue moon.**
4. Ron has a construction job. He is **a blue-collar worker.**

USE YOUR HEAD

A. Answers will vary.
B. 1. yes; 2. no; 3. no; 4. yes; 5. yes
C. 1. white-collar; 2. white-collar; 3. blue-collar; 4. blue-collar; 5. blue-collar; 6. white-collar; 7. blue-collar; 8. white-collar

PLAY IT BY EAR

1. a; 2. c; 3. b

TAPESCRIPT:

Situation 1

M: "My job is very demanding. There are always so many things to do. I only take a day off work **once in a blue moon.**"

Situation 2

W: "My grandfather worked most of his life at the factory. He used to fix machines there. He kept his job as a mechanic until he was 65 years old."

Situation 3

W: "Karen and I were really good friends in high school but I hadn't heard from her in years. Then **out of the blue,** *I got a letter from her."*

ADDITIONAL PRACTICE

See photocopiable on page 51.

Review (Lessons 16–20)

A. 1. F; 2. T; 3. T; 4. F; 5. T; 6. F; 7. F; 8. F; 9. T; 10. F

B. 1. d; 2. a; 3. b; 4. a; 5. c

C. 1. no; 2. yes; 3. no; 4. yes; 5. no; 6. no; 7. no; 8. yes

Unit Two Review

1. **on the ball**; 2. **up my alley**; 3. **out of the blue**; 4. **spill the beans**; 5. **a feather in your cap**; 6. **lose your shirt**; 7. **once in a blue moon**; 8. **throw in the towel**; 9. **a white lie**; 10. **a fish out of water**; 11. **at the drop of a hat**; 12. **rings a bell**; 13. **hot under the collar**; 14. **green with envy**; 15. **keep it under your hat**; 16. **in the long run**; 17. **got the picture**; 18. **a blue-collar worker**; 19. **on a shoestring**; 20. **in the black**

Lessons 21–30

GET THE PICTURE

1. Cindy knew she would be **in hot water** for missing her curfew.
2. Ernie tried to **break the ice** by telling a joke.
3. "I don't think Harold is right for the choir. His strange haircut is just **the tip of the iceberg.**"

USE YOUR HEAD

A. 1. yes; 2. no; 3. no; 4. yes; 5. yes
B. 2, 3, 5
C. 1. economic; 2. environmental; 3. crime
D. Answers will vary.

PLAY IT BY EAR

1. F; 2. T; 3. T

TAPESCRIPT:

Situation 1
W: "There were lots of people at the party, but nobody was talking, so I decided to tell a joke to **break the ice.**"

Situation 2
M: "Victor came to class late three days this week. Now he's **in hot water** *with his teacher."*

Situation 3
W: "Unemployment rose 4% this year, but that's just **the tip of the iceberg.** *We are facing serious economic problems."*

ADDITIONAL PRACTICE

See photocopiable on page 52.

GET THE PICTURE

1. "I think I'll have to **take a raincheck.** Let's go out another time."
2. "You look a bit **under the weather.**"
3. Felix was **a fair-weather friend.**

USE YOUR HEAD

A. 1. yes; 2. no; 3. no; 4. yes; 5. no
B. Answers will vary.
C. 2, 3, 4
D. 1. Answers will vary. (Part 1 could include: *Will there still be a party? Will you be able to drive me to work?*, etc. Part 2 could include: *Are you all right? Is your car badly damaged? How can I help you?* etc.)

PLAY IT BY EAR

1. b; 2. c; 3. a

TAPESCRIPT:

Situation 1
M: "I decided not to go out today because I'm feeling **under the weather.** *I hope I feel better tomorrow."*

Situation 2
W: "I don't trust Janet. She's **a fair-weather friend.** *She's never around when you need her."*

Situation 3
M: "I was going to have dinner with my friend but I have a big essay that I have to finish for tomorrow's class. I called my friend and told her I'd have to **take a raincheck.**"

ADDITIONAL PRACTICE

See photocopiable on page 52.

Lesson 23

GET THE PICTURE

1. Jerome wasn't sure where to go next. His plans were **up in the air.**
2. Helen always had **her feet on the ground.**
3. Doug has always had **his head in the clouds.**

USE YOUR HEAD

A. 1. **feet on the ground;** 2. **head in the clouds;** 3. **feet on the ground;** 4. **head in the clouds**
B. Answers will vary.
C. 1. Yes; 2. Yes; 3. No; 4. Yes; 5. No
D. Answers will vary.

PLAY IT BY EAR

1. no; 2. yes; 3. no

TAPESCRIPT:

Conversation 1
W2: Hey, I heard you got a job offer in San Francisco. Is that right?
W1: Well, yeah...
W2: So, have you decided whether or not you are going to move to San Francisco?
W1: Not yet. Right now, it's still **up in the air.**
1. Has the woman decided to move to San Francisco?

Conversation 2
M: My two sons are very different.
W: Why do you say that?
M: Well, my older son has his **feet on the ground.** *He has a good job and is planning for his future.*
W: What about your younger son?
M: Oh, he's got his **head in the clouds.** *He wants to be a rock star.*
2. Does the man think his older son is a sensible person?
Does the man think his younger son is a sensible person?

ADDITIONAL PRACTICE

See photocopiable on page 53.

GET THE PICTURE

1. Nancy often **made a mountain out of a molehill.**
2. Life was **a bed of roses** for Carl.
3. Larry's boss never **beat around the bush.**
4. Sometimes George felt his job was **a bed of thorns.**

USE YOUR HEAD

A. 1. **a bed of thorns;** 2. **a bed of roses;** 3. **a bed of roses;** 4. **a bed of thorns**
B. 1, 3, 5
C. Answers will vary.
D. 1. T; 2. T; 3. F; 4. T; 5. F

PLAY IT BY EAR

1. b; 2. a; 3. a

TAPESCRIPT:

Conversation 1
W2: Did you talk to Mary last night?
W1: Yes, but I still don't really know what happened. All she did was **beat around the bush.**
1. What did Mary do?

Conversation 2
M1: Your wife looks angry. What happened?
M2: Nothing that important. She's mad because I forgot to return her library book. If you ask me, she's **making a mountain out of a molehill.** *I'm going to return the book tomorrow.*
2. How does the husband feel?

Conversation 3
W1: So, how's life in the country?
W2: Much better. It's so quiet and relaxing. Really, living in the country is **a bed of roses** *compared to living in the city.*
3. How is life in the country for Gail?

ADDITIONAL PRACTICE

See photocopiable on page 53.

GET THE PICTURE

1. "Winning this should be **a piece of cake.**"
2. Football was not Derrick's **cup of tea.**
3. Shelley looked at the competition and thought, "I **bit off more than I can chew.**"

USE YOUR HEAD

A. Answers will vary.
B. 1. yes; 2. no; 3. yes; 4. no
C. Answers will vary.

PLAY IT BY EAR

1. b; 2. a; 3. c

TAPESCRIPT:

Situation 1
W: "I thought the chemistry course was going to be **over my head,** *but it turned out to be really easy."*

Situation 2
M: "I'd love to take a cooking class with you. I'm sure it's something I would enjoy doing."

Situation 3
W: "Since I had to work on the weekends. I shouldn't have take five courses this semester. It was too much for me."

ADDITIONAL PRACTICE

See photocopiable on page 54.

A. 1. yes; 2. yes; 3. yes; 4. yes; 5. no; 6. yes; 7. yes; 8. no

B. 1. c; 2. a; 3. b; 4. a; 5. d

C. 1. f; 2. e; 3. b; 4. c; 5. a; 6. d

GET THE PICTURE

1. "You **hit the nail on the head** when you said these hats would be popular."
2. "You **missed the mark** when you said this would be relaxing."
3. The movie had Billy **on the edge of his seat.**

USE YOUR HEAD

A. Answers will vary.
B. 1. **hit the nail on the head;** 2. **missed the mark;** 3. **hit the nail on the head**
C. **on the edge of my seat; missed the mark; hit the nail on the head**
D. Answers will vary.

PLAY IT BY EAR

1. b; 2. c; 3. a

TAPESCRIPT:

Conversation 1
M: *You look tired, Sally!*
W: *I am! I was up all night working on this physics problem. Just when I thought I had the answer I realized I was completely wrong.*
1. How did Sally do?

Conversation 2
W: *I heard your son was in the finals in the tennis competition. Was it a good match?*
M: *Yes — it was very close. I was so nervous, I couldn't wait to see who would win!*
2. How did the father feel?

Conversation 3
W: *Brandon, did you study very hard for this test?*
M: *Well...yes.*
W: *I thought so! You were the only student in the class who got the answers perfectly right.*
3. How did Brandon do?

ADDITIONAL PRACTICE

See photocopiable on page 54.

GET THE PICTURE

1. "If you think you're going to get a cappucino here, you're **barking up the wrong tree.**"
2. "My son is **a chip off the old block.**"
3. Marsha really **hit the roof** when she saw the mess.

USE YOUR HEAD

A. Answers will vary.
B. 1. no; 2. yes; 3. no; 4. yes; 5. yes
C. 1, 5
D. 1. yes; 2. yes; 3. no; 4. no; 5. no; 6. no

PLAY IT BY EAR

1. yes; 2. no; 3. yes

TAPESCRIPT:

Conversation 1

M: *Who did you ask to help you fix your computer?*
W: *I asked Nate Taylor.*
M: *Why did you ask him? He doesn't know anything about computers!*
1. Was the woman **barking up the wrong tree?**

Conversation 2

M: *I lost my father's favorite watch. I've looked all over, but I can't find it.*
W: *Was it the one your mother gave him for his birthday?*
M: *Yeah.*
W: *What did he do when you told him?*
M: *He was really understanding. He said that it could happen to anyone.*
2. Did the man's father **hit the roof?**

Conversation 3

W: *Doesn't Dick remind you of his father, Dr. Brody?*
M: *He sure does. They are alike in so many ways.*
W: *I wasn't at all surprised when he said that he wanted to go to medical school.*
3. Is Dick **a chip off the old block?**

ADDITIONAL PRACTICE

See photocopiable on page 55.

Lesson 28

GET THE PICTURE

1. Everyone was there to see Jack and Rosie **tie the knot.**
2. "**In a nutshell,** the monkey did it. That's all I have to say."
3. "You need to learn how to **take it easy.**"

USE YOUR HEAD

A. 1. yes; 2. no; 3. yes; 4. no; 5. no
B. 1. Newport, Rhode Island; 2. Saturday, June 9; 3. New York City
C. Answers will vary. (Could include *watching TV, reading a book, taking a nap, playing sports, drinking some coffee,* etc.)
D. Answers will vary.

PLAY IT BY EAR

1. in July; 2. They wanted to make sure it was true love; 3. They are going to Hawaii to relax.

TAPESCRIPT:

W1: Ruth and Marty have been dating for ten years and they finally decided to **tie the knot** *in July.*
W2: I wonder why they waited for so long.
W1: There were a lot of reasons, but **in a nutshell,** *I guess they wanted to make sure it was true love.*
W2: What are they going to do for their honeymoon?
W1: They both have stressful jobs, so they want to go to Hawaii and just **take it easy** *for a few weeks.*

1. When are Ruth and Marty getting married?
2. Why did Ruth and Marty wait so long to get married?
3. What are Ruth and Marty going to do for their honeymoon?

ADDITIONAL PRACTICE

See photocopiable on page 55.

GET THE PICTURE

1. "I think I'll **take my time.** I'm in no hurry."
2. Cowboy Will decided to leave town **on the spur of the moment.**
3. "I can teach you how to catch a fly **in no time flat.**"

USE YOUR HEAD

A. 2; 4
B. 2; 3; 5
C. Answers will vary.
D. Answers will vary.

PLAY IT BY EAR

1. b; 2. a; 3. c

TAPESCRIPT:

Situation 1
M: "I was a little worried about the project. When we started, there seemed to be so much work to do but everyone on the committee really worked together, and they finished it very quickly."

Situation 2
W: "Some people can write their essays really quickly but not me! I find it's better not to hurry too much. Then I don't make a lot of mistakes."

Situation 3
W: "I'm one of those people who can make quick decisions. For example, there was my holiday in San Diego. I didn't plan to go there. I just thought about it one morning and left that afternoon."

ADDITIONAL PRACTICE

See photocopiable on page 56.

GET THE PICTURE

1. "I think we **missed the boat** on getting into this movie."
2. "What should we do? Looks like we're all **in the same boat.**"
3. "Do you have any money? I'm **broke.**"

USE YOUR HEAD

A. 1. yes; 2. yes; 3. no
B. Answers will vary.
C. 1. yes; 2. no; 3. yes
D. Answers will vary.

PLAY IT BY EAR

1. b; 2. a; 3. c

TAPESCRIPT:

Conversation 1

W: Hi Tom. A few of us are going to a concert tomorrow night. Do you want to come?
M: Oh sorry, I can't. I have to be very careful for the rest of the month. I won't have any money until I get my next paycheck.

Conversation 2

W1: You know, when I first came to the United States, I didn't know very much English.
W2: Me neither. I felt quite nervous at the beginning.
W1: Yes. I know exactly what you mean.

Conversation 3

M1: Did Alice get the tickets for the show?
M2: No! She waited too long to make reservations. When she got to the theater, all the tickets were already sold out.
M1: Oh. That's too bad.

ADDITIONAL PRACTICE

See photocopiable on page 56.

Review Lessons 26–30

A. 1. no; 2. yes; 3. no; 4. yes; 5. no; 6. no; 7. no; 8. no; 9. no; 10. no

B. 1. **missed the boat;** 2. **take it easy;** 3. **in no time flat;** 4. **tie the knot;** 5. **hit the nail on the head;** 6. **barking up the wrong tree;** 7. **a chip off the old block;** 8. **take my time;** 9. **on the edge of my seat;** 10. **hit the roof**

C. 1. I'm **broke;** 2. he's **a chip off the old block;** 3. I'll be finished **in no time flat;** 4. I **hit the roof;** 5. I **took my time;** 6. I **missed the boat.**

Unit Three Review

1. **up in the air;** 2. **in a nutshell;** 3. **a bed of roses;** 4. **in the same boat;** 5. **tie the knot;** 6. **take a raincheck;** 7. **on the edge of my seat;** 8. **bite off more than you can chew;** 9. **beat around the bush;** 10. **on the spur of the moment;** 11. **under the weather;** 12. **my cup of tea;** 13. **a piece of cake;** 14. **make a mountain out of a molehill;** 15. **in hot water;** 16. **take it easy;** 17. **barking up the wrong tree;** 18. **a chip off the old block;** 19. **feet on the ground;** 20. **in no time flat**

Lesson 1

ADDITIONAL PRACTICE

Imagine that your friend has asked you to *keep an eye on* his/her house while he/she is away for the summer. Imagine the things you have to look after (plants, pet, car, yard, etc.) and imagine what might go right or wrong. Make a list.

_______________________'s house.

Keep an eye on... (List items)	Situation one week later (Circle one)	Explain
1.	Okay/Not Okay	
2.	Okay/Not Okay	
3.	Okay/Not Okay	
4.	Okay/Not Okay	

Write a letter to your friend to explain what happened.

Dear (Janice),

You asked me to **keep an eye on** your house while you were on holidays, so here is my report.
First of all, the (cat) is fine. It is... As well, ...is also fine...
However, I tried to **keep an eye on** your (plants) but...

Lesson 2

ADDITIONAL PRACTICE

Try to *pull your classmate's leg.* Write down three statements about yourself – two of them true and one of them false. (For example: I saw Michael Jackson in concert once./I went to Paris for holidays a few years ago./Physics is my favorite subject.)

Statement One	
Statement Two	
Statement Three	

Share your statements with your partner. Let him/her ask you questions to try to decide when you are *pulling his/her leg.* Try to convince him/her that all three stories are true.

Student A: I went to a Michael Jackson concert once.
Student B: Are you **pulling my leg?**
Student A: No, it's true. I went in 1992...

Then ask him/her questions about his/her statements.

Choose one of those statements (true or false) and write about it in a paragraph.

Would you believe that I went to Paris once? ...

End the paragraph with Am I pulling your leg? **Share your paragraph with your classmates.**

Lesson 3

ADDITIONAL PRACTICE

Imagine you have a job where you really have to be *on your toes* at all times (a police officer, a zoo keeper, an astronaut, a taxi driver, a kindergarten teacher, etc.). List what you have to watch for to be *on your toes*. Write about an exciting event that happens.

Work Report

Name: ______________________ Occupation: ______________________

Date: ______________________ Place: ______________________

Things to watch for (to be **on your toes**): ______________________

____

____

Describe an event that happens:

1. ______________________
2. ______________________
3. ______________________
4. ______________________
5. ______________________

Write a report for the local newspaper.

My name is ____________ and I'm a ______________ (occupation). I have the kind of job where you have to be **on your toes** all the time. For example, I always have to watch for...

However, even if you are **on your toes** things will happen. Yesterday is an example of that...

Lesson 4

ADDITIONAL PRACTICE

Imagine that something important has *slipped your mind* (a term paper, a date, somebody's birthday, etc.). Explain to the person involved (a teacher, boyfriend/girlfriend, mother, etc.) what happened. Explain what you can do to help solve this problem.

Who are you? (a student/employee/child, etc.) ______________________

Who is your partner? (a teacher/boss/parent, etc.) ______________________

What **slipped your mind?** ______________________

____

What's your reason? ______________________

____

What's your solution? ______________________

____

Write a letter of apology to your partner. Does he/she accept your solution?

Dear (Mr. Bromwell),

I know that my history essay was due yesterday but it completely **slipped my mind...** I am sorry but I was... Would it be possible for me to...

Lesson 5

ADDITIONAL PRACTICE

Imagine that you are a parent/teacher/friend and you are trying to encourage your child/student/friend to do his/her best. An important event is coming up soon (final tests, a big sports event, a music competition, etc.) and you want him/her to *keep his/her chin up.* Work with a partner and write a conversation.

Who are you? (a teacher, parent, friend, etc.) ______________________

Who are you talking to? (a student, child, friend, etc.) ______________________

What's happening? ______________________

____

Why does he/she need to **keep his/her chin up?** ______________________

____

What does he/she need to do? ______________________

____

Write the dialog.

Student A (parent):	When is the chemistry final?
Student B (high school student):	Next week! It's really difficult!
Student A:	Well, **keep your chin up.** This is what I think you need to do...

Lesson 6

ADDITIONAL PRACTICE

Try to think of an English song that you know *by heart* (rock song, children's song, traditional folk song, etc.). Work with your partner to write the lyrics for that song. Try to remember any other details you have about that song.

Name of song: ______________________

Name of singer/group: ______________________

Date the song became popular: ______________________

Where you first heard the song: (on the radio, a friend's CD, at school, etc.) ______________________

____

With your partner, write the lyrics for the song by heart.

____

____

____

____

If time permits, sing one verse for the class.

Lesson 7

ADDITIONAL PRACTICE

Imagine you write an advice column. Someone writes to you about a problem that really *gets on his/her nerves* (people who talk in movie theaters, noisy parties from the neighbors, people who break traffic rules, etc.). Give him/her advice. What should he/she do?

Problem

What **gets on the person's nerves?** ____________________

Where does this happen? How often? ____________________

____

Response

Do you agree that this is a serious problem? Yes ☐ No ☐

What should he/she do?

____

____

Write the question and response in letter format.

Dear Dr. Advice,

I'm writing about something that really **gets on my nerves...** What should I do?

Frustrated

Dear Frustrated,

I understand that... really **gets on your nerves...** I think you need to...

Dr. Advice

Lesson 8

ADDITIONAL PRACTICE

Imagine a problem situation that you are observing. Provide two possible responses to that situation – a *levelheaded* response and response that is not so *levelheaded*. (Follow the example in Exercise C on page 19 of the Student Book.) What happens?

Situation

Setting (Where/When does it take place?): ____________________

Characters (Who are the main people involved?): ____________________

Conflict (What is the problem?): ____________________

Response #1

What would be a **levelheaded** response? ____________________

What would be the likely result? ____________________

Response #2

What would be another response? ____________________

What would be the likely result? ____________________

Write your response (as a *levelheaded* person) in a letter to a friend.

Dear Robert,

Yesterday I was down at the beach when... I knew I should be **levelheaded** so I... As a result...

Lesson 9

ADDITIONAL PRACTICE

Imagine a Saturday when you really *have your hands full.* Write out a possible schedule with six activities. Also write down an activity you would like to do with your friend. Work with a partner and try to arrange a time to meet. Change your schedule if needed.

Name: ____________________

Plans (What would you like to do with your friend tomorrow? When?): ____________________

____

Schedule: (What are you doing tomorrow? Write down six activities.)

Time	Activities	Time	Activities
6–8 a.m.	______	4–6 p.m.	______
8–10 a.m.	______	6–8 p.m.	______
10–12 p.m.	______	8–10 p.m.	______
12–2 p.m.	______	10–12 a.m.	______
2–4 p.m.	______		

Write the dialog.

Student A: So, what are you doing tomorrow?
Student B: I'm really busy. I **have my hands full.**
Student A: I **have my hands full** too, but do you want to meet for lunch?

Lesson 10

ADDITIONAL PRACTICE

Imagine that you have the chance to meet an important person (rock star, politician, athlete, historical figure from the past, etc.) *face to face.* Who would you like to meet the most? What three questions would you ask?

Person you'd like to meet **face to face:** ____________________

Reasons why you'd like to meet him/her: ____________________

____

Questions you'd like to ask:

1. ____________________
2. ____________________
3. ____________________

Write your ideas in a paragraph.

The person I'd like to meet **face to face** the most is... I'd like to meet him/her because...

The three questions I'd ask would be:

1. ____________________
2. ____________________
3. ____________________

11 Lesson

ADDITIONAL PRACTICE

A movie director wants you for his latest movie. You'll have to quit your job/school and move to Hollywood immediately. Should you stay or go? Consider things like family, friends, money, career, adventure, etc. Make a list about what would be good or bad about each choice, *in the short run* **and** *in the long run.* **Make your decision.**

In the short run

Stay at home		Go to Hollywood	
Pros	Cons	Pros	Cons
____________	____________	____________	____________
____________	____________	____________	____________

Decision **in the short run:** Stay ☐ Go ☐

In the long run

Stay at home		Go to Hollywood	
Pros	Cons	Pros	Cons
____________	____________	____________	____________
____________	____________	____________	____________

Decision **in the long run:** Stay ☐ Go ☐

Write a letter to the director explaining your decision.

Dear Mr. Hollywood,

I have thought about your offer and have decided...

In the short run, I think...

In the long run, I think...

12 Lesson

ADDITIONAL PRACTICE

Write about the type of person (real or imaginary) who is *a team player.* **What three qualities does this person need to have? Why?**

Being ***a team player.***

List three important qualities and explain why they are important.

1. ____
____

2. ____
____

3. ____
____

Write your ideas in a paragraph.

A person who is ***a team player*** needs to have these three qualities. First of all, the person needs to be... This is because... Second of all, the person needs to be...

Lesson 13

ADDITIONAL PRACTICE

Think of something that you (or a family member or friend) has done that has been *a feather in your (his/her) cap.* Describe the accomplishment and your (his/her) feelings about it.

Who was involved? (You/Your friend/Your sister, etc.) ______________________

When did this happen? ______________________

Where did it happen? ______________________

What happened? (Explain) ______________________

____

____

Why was this **a feather in your (his/her) cap?** ______________________

____

____

Write your ideas in a paragraph.

(Learning how to ski) was **a feather in my cap...**

Lesson 14

ADDITIONAL PRACTICE

Imagine you are planning a three-day holiday *on a shoestring* budget. What could you do? Where could you go? Decide how much money you have to spend and how you will spend it. (Think about accommodation, food, travel, souvenirs, etc.)

Budget: (Remember you are **on a shoestring.**) ______________________

Where will you go? ______________________

Expenses:	Item	Cost
Day One	______	______
	______	______
Day Two	______	______
	______	______
Day Three	______	______
	______	______

Total Cost ______________________

Did you keep to your budget? Yes ☐ No ☐

Write your ideas in a paragraph.

It's possible (not possible) to (go camping) **on a shoestring** budget...

15 Lesson

ADDITIONAL PRACTICE

Imagine something exciting has just happened. *Give someone a ring* **and tell him/her about it. Work with a partner.**

What happened? ____________________

____

When? ____________________

Where? ____________________

How do you feel about it? ____________________

____

____

Who do you **give a ring** to? ____________________

How does he/she feel about it? ____________________

Write your ideas in a phone conversation to a friend.

Student A: Hello! You'll never guess what happened! I had to **give you a ring!!**

Student B: ...

16 Lesson

ADDITIONAL PRACTICE

Think about an activity or job that is right *up your alley.* **Describe what you like about it.**

Name of activity/job	What does it include?	What do you enjoy about that?

Write your ideas in a paragraph.

(Hiking in the mountains) is really **up my alley...**

Lesson 17

ADDITIONAL PRACTICE

Write a newspaper article about something wonderful happening that has someone *walking on air.* (It could be true or imaginary.)

Who? (Who is the main character?) ______
What? (What happened?) ______
When? ______
Where? ______
Why? (Why was it so special?) ______
Other details: ______
______
______
Quote from person: ______
______

Write your ideas in a newspaper article.

(Johnny Thiessen) was **walking on air** last night...

Lesson 18

ADDITIONAL PRACTICE

You are going to open a business. You hope to be *in the black* within a year. What kind of business will you open? Where will you open it? What are three ways you can help make your business a success?

Type of business: ______
______
Location: ______
Description: What will help your business succeed?
1. ______
______
2. ______
______
3. ______
______

Write your ideas in a report.

I plan to open a business and have it **in the black** within a year. The business is...

19 Lesson

ADDITIONAL PRACTICE

Describe the events of a *red-letter day* involving you and/or family and friends. What made this day so special?

Event: ______________________

When: ______________________

Where: ______________________

Describe what happened. (What made it special?) ______________________

____

____

____

____

Write your ideas in a paragraph.

July 31, 1996 was **a red-letter day** for my family. That was the day that...

20 Lesson

ADDITIONAL PRACTICE

Describe an activity that you do (or a place that you go to) *once in a blue moon*. Would you like to do this (or go there) more often? Why or why not?

Activity (or Place): ______________________

Describe (What is it like?): ______________________

____

____

Would you like to do that (go there) more often? Yes ☐ No ☐

Why (or why not)? ______________________

____

____

Write your ideas in a paragraph.

Once in a blue moon, I (go bowling)...

Lesson 21

ADDITIONAL PRACTICE

Imagine you write an advice column. Someone writes to tell you he/she is *in hot water* with another person for some reason (being late for an appointment, losing or damaging something that belongs to him/her, forgetting to invite him/her to a party, etc.). Give him/her some advice.

Who is he/she **in hot water** with? ______________________

Why is he/she **in hot water?** ______________________

____

Response

What should he/she do? ______________________

____

____

Write the question and response in letter format.

Dear Dr. Advice,

I'm really **in hot water** with my friend...

In Hot Water

Dear In Hot Water,

I can understand why you are **in hot water...** I think you should...

Dr. Advice

Lesson 22

ADDITIONAL PRACTICE

It's a Sunday morning and you're feeling a bit *under the weather.* What are three things you could do to make you feel better?

List three possible "cures" for someone who is feeling **under the weather.**

Do you think each would work? Why or why not?

1. ______________________

____

2. ______________________

____

3. ______________________

____

Write your ideas in a diary entry.

Dear Diary,

I woke up this morning feeling a bit **under the weather.** I wanted to feel better, so the first thing I did was...

23 Lesson

ADDITIONAL PRACTICE

Write about twin brothers or sisters. One has *his/her feet on the ground* **and the other** *has his/her head in the clouds.* **Imagine them planning a holiday together. Choose a destination. Decide what each would like to do at that place. How do they plan their holiday?**

Destination (Where are they going?): ______________________

What would he/she like to do there?

Person A **(feet on the ground)** ______________________

____

____

Person B **(head in the clouds)** ______________________

____

____

Write a postcard (from either twin) to a friend describing the holiday.

Dear (Sarah),

I'm here (in Paris) on my holidays with (Don). As you know, I'm the one with **my feet on the ground** so I've been... However, Don has **his head in the clouds** and is...

24 Lesson

ADDITIONAL PRACTICE

Your life is *a bed of roses.* **Describe what you do. (This can be true or imaginary.)**

Name: ______________________

Occupation: ______________________

Address: ______________________

What makes your life **a bed of roses?** Describe five things that make your life great.

1. ______________________
2. ______________________
3. ______________________
4. ______________________
5. ______________________

Write your ideas in a letter.

Dear (Susan),

My life is truly **a bed of roses...**

Lesson 25

ADDITIONAL PRACTICE

Think of an everyday activity that's *a piece of cake* for you (tying your shoes, taking the subway, checking your email, etc.). Imagine describing how to do this activity to someone who has never done this before. Write down all the steps. Practice with your partner. Does he/she understand your instructions?

Activity: ______________________________

Procedures (How do you do this?):

1. ______________________________
2. ______________________________
3. ______________________________
4. ______________________________
5. ______________________________
6. ______________________________

Write your ideas in a report.

Tying your shoes is **a piece of cake.** The first thing you have to do is... Next... After that... Finally...

Lesson 26

ADDITIONAL PRACTICE

Imagine that you are a TV reporter. You are covering an event that has you *on the edge of your seat* (a sports event, an election, a movie, a space launch, etc.). Describe what happens. Write about how you feel.

Event: ______________________________

When: ______________________________

Where: ______________________________

Why are you **on the edge of your seat?**

What happens? ______________________________

____

How do you feel? ______________________________

____

____

Write your ideas in a TV report.

This is (Brad Fitzgerald) reporting for CTG News. I'm reporting from the tennis courts where I'm really **on the edge of my seat** watching...

Lesson 27

ADDITIONAL PRACTICE

Think about something that makes you *hit the roof* (noisy dogs, traffic jams, poor service in a restaurant or store, etc.). Describe why this makes you angry. What can done to solve the problem? Write a letter to the editor of a newspaper explaining the problem.

Problem (What makes you **hit the roof?**): ______________________

____

Why does it make you angry? ______________________

____

Solution (What can be done?): ______________________

____

____

____

Write your ideas in a letter to the editor of a newspaper.

Dear Sir/Madam,

Traffic jams in this city really make me **hit the roof...** I think we need to...

Lesson 28

ADDITIONAL PRACTICE

Write about a couple you know that has *tied the knot*. When did they get married? Give details about the wedding.

Who **tied the knot?** ______________________

When did they get married? ______________________

Where did they get married? ______________________

How many people attended? ______________________

Other details: ______________________

____

____

Write your ideas in a paragraph.

My friends (Jane Smith and Doug Lee) **tied the knot** last July...

Lesson 29

ADDITIONAL PRACTICE

What kind of holiday do you prefer – a holiday where you *take your time* and have everything carefully organized or a holiday where you decide everything *on the spur of the moment?* Write about the good and bad points of both types of holidays. Describe which type of holiday is the best for you.

	Pros	Cons
Holiday #1 (**take your time** to organize)		
Holiday #2 (decide **on the spur of the moment**)		
Check which holiday is the best for you. Holiday #1 ☐ Holiday #2 ☐		

Write about your ideas in a paragraph.

I like the kind of holiday where I can **take my time** (or decide things **on the spur of the moment**)... The good points about this kind of holiday are that... The bad points are that...

Overall, I think...

Lesson 30

ADDITIONAL PRACTICE

Imagine that you and your friend are both *broke.* Plan a fun Sunday for yourselves. Fill out the schedule and then send an email to your friend suggesting plans.

Schedule: Saturday

Time	Activities	Cost
6–8 a.m.		
8–10 a.m.		
10–12 p.m.		
12–2 p.m.		
2–4 p.m.		
6–8 p.m.		
8–10 p.m.		

Write an email message to your friend.

Dear Sandy,

I have some ideas for Sunday. I know we're both **broke,** so I was thinking...